The Spiritual Journey

Mountain Tops, Dark Nights, and Dangerous Deception

Dr. Bill Atwood

Ekklesia Publications
Carrollton, Texas

The Spiritual Journey
Mountain Tops, Dark Nights, and Dangerous Deception

ISBN 978-0-9889552-4-0

Published by Ekklesia Publications

Printed in the United States of America

For all book orders:
www.ekk.org

For Information:
Ekklesia Publications • P. O. Box 118526 • Carrollton, Texas 75011-8526

Table of Contents

Dedication

At a time when I was spiritually raw, I met a Roman Catholic lay woman who was a licensed therapist trained in Spiritual Direction by Sam Anthony Morello, O.C.D. an expert on the Carmelite order. She had a great fondness for wolves and the dynamics of a wolf pack. Wolf packs exhibit amazing social order and healthy relationships within their extended family. When I shared about the agonies I was going through and how badly I felt about them, she gave me a dismissive wave and said, "Oh, honey, you just want to be closer to God."

That comment started conversations that spanned over many years, as she shared about the spiritual journey as a spiral and we revisit the same issues at deeper and deeper levels.

I am deeply indebted to Kaye Briscoe King for her insights and heart for the Gospel, the Kingdom, and the Lord. This book is dedicated to her— because she never got around to writing her version of it! (or at least was never satisfied with what she had written).

Thanks, Mom Wolf!

Acknowledgements

This small book would have been impossible to write without the work that was done by St. John of the Cross and Theresa of Avila. I am also in the debt of Kaye Briscoe King for her insights and the Rev. Lee Ligon-Borden, Ph. D., for her patient and tireless editing.

Preface

Spiritual Journey or Dangerous Deception

One of the remarkable insights revealed in the book of the prophet Isaiah is the fact that, although God created billions of us, he looks on every person as an individual:

> "I, the LORD, search the heart, I test the mind, Even to give every man according to his ways, according to the fruit of his doings."[1]

Each one of us has a story to tell, and each one is on a spiritual journey. Whereas details often are unique in each person's walk, certain hallmarks of the journey along the way are, more often than not, shared. St. John of the Cross and St. Teresa of Avila spoke about this common bond in their writings in the 16th century. Since then, many others have as well, but the concept of a spiritual journey has not been shared and embraced anywhere nearly enough. Knowledge of the journey's different aspects would help mitigate the suffering of many people as their individual circumstances, the Holy Spirit, and even their own heart's cry work to help them be conformed to the character of Christ.[2]

I had never run across much of a contemporary systematic approach to "The Journey" until meeting Kaye Briscoe King, a Roman Catholic lay woman who was given a remarkable insight. She was well trained in spiritual direction by Anthony Morello, who was at the time the spiritual director of the Carmelites. They both had embraced and followed the writings of John of the Cross and St. Teresa. Kaye had the wonderful insight of the journey as a spiral whereby we pass through the same spiritual regions several times at different levels while we move closer in union with Christ.

As I mentioned in the Dedication, my first substantive encounter with Kaye was in sharing heart-wrenching pain over the sense of my own failures and sins. Hardly able to bear ministry and other pains of life, I asked her how one could go on when burdened by so much baggage and spiritual duplicity. Her answer was life-changing. She simply said,

---

[1] Isaiah 17:10
[2] Romans 8:29, II Corinthians 3:18

"Honey, you just want to be closer to God, that's all."

The idea that poignant awareness of sin and mixed motives in my life, after decades of Christian service and even ordained ministry, could mean that I was making progress, rather than simply failing, was a revolution.

During the next several years, as I began to learn about spiritual direction and the journey, I discovered the value of this wonderful model of the journey as a spiral. The reason it is so profound is that it magnificently describes the way in which issues can be re-visited in a person's life as they grow in Christ. At first, we will be dealing with external behavior. Eventually, the Holy Spirit will challenge our motives and the condition of our hearts. We may still be dealing with selfishness or pride, but the level of the dealing will be ever deeper as we move along the journey toward union with God in Christ. This book is an attempt to share something of the insights of the journey as a spiral and to help identify some of the landmarks along the way. It is not intended so much to help identify where one is at a given time — that is actually quite difficult to do without outside help. Nor is it particularly important to do so. Instead, there are two great challenges and truths: *First*, am I willing to take whatever "next step" God is asking me to take? *Second*, can I believe, even in the midst of my pain and struggle, that there is something more ahead that is good and spiritually rewarding? In fact, do I believe that union with God in Christ is really possible?

The classic language of the spiritual journey speaks of traversing from pre-purgative, through the purgative way, the illuminative way, and into the unitive way. Those terms seem to be as good as any, but much of the formal language of spiritual direction seems to be an unnecessary obstacle. It is sad to see people who are overwhelmed by the historic form of terms such as *Ascent of Mt. Carmel* or *Interior Castles*. While not attempting to replace those works in any way, this book is an attempt to provide an introduction to the interior life and the spiritual journey. It is my fervent hope that it will spark interest in the historic works that have shaped many people's lives for centuries.

Bill Atwood
Carrollton, Texas
May, 2014

SECTION ONE

THE PRE-PURGATIVE WAY

CHAPTER ONE

The Pre-Purgative Way

Alive Yet Dead

The awful fruit of the Garden where sin was born is that every person in every generation is born separated from God. Although He has created us and known us, we do not know Him. Purgation comes from the Latin *pugare*, to be purged or cleansed. The ***Pre-purgative Way*** simply refers to life before the process of purging begins. When we are pre-purgative, we have not yet begun our own journey.

When the Lord God formed man from the dust of the ground, He breathed into him the breath of life, and man became a living soul. In a beautiful mirroring of the Trinity of God, we are created in trinity as well with a body, a soul, and a spirit. Originally, God breathed in the breath of His spirit, and it took up residence in the human spirit. One might imagine the human spirit being like a balloon in which the breath, or spirit, of God resided. When the first humans chose to disobey God, a great wound was inflicted on the human spirit...like air that is lost when puncturing a balloon, so the Spirit within blew away.

When Adam and Eve were commanded not to eat of the fruit of the tree of the knowledge of good and evil, they were expressly told that if they did, in that day they would "surely die."[1] Since they continued in physical life, one must assume that the "dying" was of another sort, and it was. It was spiritual death. Now, even if God breathes on us again, He cannot take up residence inside us again until the spirit is healed. That happens when we come to Him in faith.

That is our natural state at birth. Even before we have the chance to plot how to get to the cookie jar before dinner or think of ways to transgress boundaries because it seems nice at the time, we are

---

[1] Genesis 2:17

already under the weight of sin. That burden is called *original sin*. Whether or not we have intentionally chosen a sin *action* (which everyone does), even before that, we have a sin *problem* that causes us to fall short of the demands of holiness.

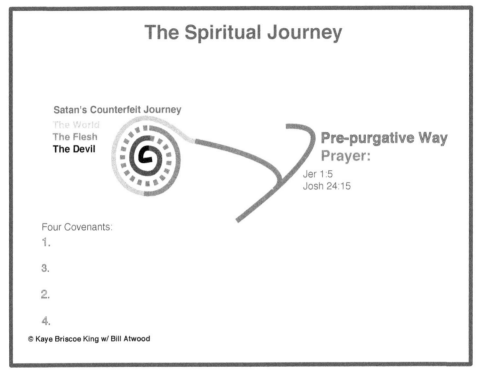

Until that problem is fixed, we are incapable of spiritual action. That limitation   certainly does not mean we are incapable of religion. Religion is the magnificent fruit of the human soul and is lived out in the body, but it does *not* mean that there is anything spiritual about it at all. Before our spirits are healed, before we come to life in Christ, we are still capable of performing many religious acts. We can pray liturgical prayers, cross ourselves, sing hymns, and even go to seminary and be ordained. However, apart from our spirits being healed and starting a new life in Christ, we will always come up short. Sadly, many churches never tell people about the redeeming love of Christ or that they can be spiritually healed. Jesus talked about this as being born "from above" or "born again."[2]

While that language has become common in Evangelical circles and often is attributed to the Baptist, there is a great deal of confusion about it, and there are a great many questions about it.

---

[2] John 3:7

The fact remains, however, that it is not a Baptist doctrine; it is a Christian one, and we need to understand what it means.

The Pre-purgative Way is marked, then, by external religious behavior (if there is any attempt at all to relate with God). We can engage in all sorts of "religious" activities that look good, but that is not what God ultimately had in mind for us. He desires that we come to know the union that He has with the Spirit and the Son.[3]

At some point, people begin to come into an awareness that something is missing, and they hunger for something more. Blaise Pascal said that the hunger remains, "because the infinite abyss can only be filled by an infinite and immutable object, that is to say, only by God Himself."[4]

St. Augustine said something similar: "Thou hast made us for thyself, O Lord, and our hearts are restless until they find their rest in thee."[5] Certainly, that awareness can come at a very young age for some people, but the point is that it is not automatic. Many of us live for decades and never come to the realization that Jesus wants to be real in our lives.

First Covenant – "I Will Journey with You, Jesus"

As we are becoming aware of this hunger, we are called to our *first covenant* with Jesus. He asks us if we will come with Him, and we say, "I will journey with You, Jesus." That does not mean we have arrived spiritually, of course; it simply means we have intentionally begun.

In the book about her life, St. Teresa records her first steps in prayer at the point of her conversion:

> This is the method of prayer I then used: since I could not reflect discursively with the intellect, I strove to picture Christ within me, and it did me greater good— in my opinion—to picture Him in those scenes where I saw Him more alone. It seemed to me that being alone and afflicted, as a person in need, He had to accept me.[6]

---

[3] John 17:3
[4] Blaise Pascal, *Pensees*, Translated by W. F. Trotter, p. 425
 http://oregonstate.edu/instruct/phl302/texts/pascal/pensees- a.html
[5] *Augustine's Confessions, Book One, Chapter 1.1*, Translated by Dr. Albert C. Outler, SMU [pdf available here:
http://www.ccel.org/a/augustine/confessions/confessions.html]
[6] *The Collected Works of St. Teresa of Avila*, Vol. 1, *The Book of Her Life, Spiritual Testimonies, and Soliloquies*, Translated by Kieran Kavanaugh and Otilio Rodriguez (Washington, DC: Institute of Carmelite Studies, 1976) 9:4

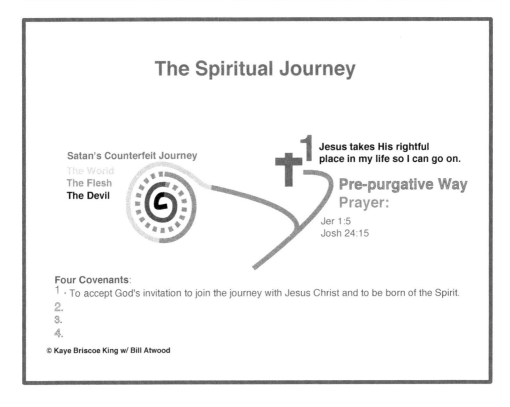

The Spiritual Journey

Satan's Counterfeit Journey
The World
The Flesh
The Devil

Jesus takes His rightful
place in my life so I can go on.

Pre-purgative Way
Prayer:
Jer 1:5
Josh 24:15

Four Covenants:
1 . To accept God's invitation to join the journey with Jesus Christ and to be born of the Spirit.
2.
3.
4.

© Kaye Briscoe King w/ Bill Atwood

We begin our spiritual journey by saying "Yes" to God and to the pattern of His kingdom. Unregenerate, human flesh has strong convictions about how we should proceed in life. The focus is on oneself and gratifying the hungers found in our life. The lure of the flesh is a false hope that there is an easy, painless way to come to abundant life. However, instead of being able to satisfy the hunger inside, the flesh starts out sweetly, but it quickly turns bitter. By contrast, the Kingdom demands a great price for entry. The challenge of the Kingdom can be very intimidating. A price must be paid before we can receive the treasure. Of course, the price is infinitely more costly to Jesus than it is to us, but our flesh complains all the same. We really want to believe the lie that we can get something for nothing, that we can just take a step into some kind of fairyland and get what we want and what we need.

In reality, this is one of the great principles of the Kingdom: positive moral choices have a short-term negative result before the positive result is received in the long run, whereas negative moral choices have consequences that appear in the short run to be positive but have long-term negative consequences. There is "pleasure in sin for a season,"[7] is true, but the ultimate harvest cannot be avoided.

At this point of making a decision to follow Jesus, everything changes. The power of being born "from above" or "born again" is released. We begin to realize the promise that God offered to us in baptism. (Or for those who are now baptized, that God offers at that time.) We are just beginning to walk with Him, but we may well think we have arrived. Where there was no life before, now life is in Technicolor! Where once there was emptiness, a great fullness rises up. It is exciting beyond anything the world can offer. In our enthusiasm, it is easy to overdo our sharing about what has happened. The transformation is so great that many people say new converts should be locked up for six months!

For the first time, we are beginning to experience Christ. We are coming to know Him about whom we have only heard second-hand. There is a wonderful sense of wholeness as we become aware of God living in us by the power of His Spirit.

Now, we enter The Purgative Way

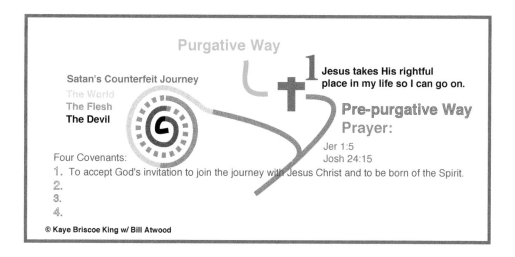

© Kaye Briscoe King w/ Bill Atwood

---

[7] Hebrews 11:25

Application

1.   Was there a point in time when, or a season during which, a personal relationship with Jesus Christ became real for you? If so, could you share about that?

a.   What was your life like before coming into a relationship with Jesus Christ? How would you characterize it? What were your main priorities?

b.   What happened as your relationship with Him came to life? What were the circumstances that brought you to an awareness of your need to have Jesus Christ in your life?

c.   What is your life like now?

2.   If you have *not* yet come into a personal relationship with Jesus Christ, would you like to enter into a personal relationship now? You can do that by praying an invitation something like this:

Lord Jesus Christ, thank you for loving me. Thank you for inviting me into a relationship of purpose. I ask You now to enter into my life, forgiving my sins and giving me new life. Please help my relationship with You grow and prosper. Lead me to a church that is rooted in your Word (the Bible) and is a faithful body of believers seeking to know You and be faithful to You. Help me along the way as I journey with You and seek to be more like You.

SECTION TWO

THE PURGATIVE WAY

CHAPTER TWO

The Kingdom of God – The Purgative Way

Beyond the Mountaintop

The *Purgative Way* also gets its name from the Latin term *pugare* (to purge). It is so named because it is the period of time during which we *consciously* begin cooperating with the process of being cleansed (or purged) of sin. The Spiritual Journey is an ongoing process that takes a lifetime, but this is its beginning. At this initial step, we enter into the first of four key covenants with God.

Many different factors can lead up to this first covenant commitment, which essentially involves simply saying "Yes," to God. Specifically, it is a decision that says, "Yes, I choose to respond to Your love and journey with You." As we begin, we don't know much about what will come, but we will know that we have begun to walk with Christ.

The confidence of a new believer generally is very strong. God usually rewards our new commitment to Christ with an almost overwhelming sense of joy. It is often called a *"mountaintop experience"* because it feels like we are on top of the world. Many people think, "This is what I was made for," and immediately try to get everyone else to join their spot on the mountain. In a sense, it is true. We were made for fellowship with God. The mistake we make is in thinking that the new relationship will stay the same indefinitely. Because the new believer's experience of God is so limited, it is a natural mistake, but it is a mistake all the same. It would be like saying, "Education is complete now that I have enrolled," "A meal should be a perpetual *hors d'oeuvre*," or "The first kiss at the wedding fulfills the marriage."

Obviously, all of these examples show the foolishness of such thinking. The mountain is sweet, though. St. Teresa described it this way:

> Great is this favor, my Spouse; a pleasing feast. Precious wine do You give me, for with one drop alone You make me forget all of creation and go out from creat5ures and myself, so that I will no longer want the joys and comforts that my sensuality desired up until now. Great is this favor; I did not deserve it.[10]

---

[10] *St. Teresa*, vol. 2, 4:6

Another common misconception of new believers is assuming that everyone who is not happily enjoying the mountaintop experience is, very regrettably, in the wrong place – or is not even a Christian. They try to goad their pre-purgative friends to join them by saying, "You just don't know what you are missing!" To those who are in different places in the journey, they say, "You don't have to miss out on this wonderful feeling. Come back to the mountaintop. It is what you were made for."

It is what church consultant Carl George calls the "Doctrine of Plausibility." If something seems reasonable, it *seems* that it *must* be so. If it will "preach," so much the better, even if it is not provable or true. But it is not necessarily so. In this case, it is not the mountaintop that God wants to see developed in our lives; rather, it is the character of Christ. Like coffee beans that are of no use if they stay on the mountainside, we need to move beyond that phase of life and grow spiritually. That growth can occur only as some significant changes take place. Just as coffee beans need to be roasted, ground, and scalded with hot water in order for their true character to be released, it is the rigors of the journey that really shape and release grace in our lives:

> ...but we also glory in tribulations, knowing that tribulation produces perseverance; and perseverance, character; and character, hope. Now hope does not disappoint, because the love of God has been poured out in our hearts by the Holy Spirit who was given to us.[11]

Because He loves us and is committed to the formation of our character, God helps us along the way. After rewarding us with the electrifying sense of His presence, the next step is to move us into the first "Dark Night," as John of the Cross calls it.

This "Active Dark Night of the Senses" is a time when God withdraws the sense of His presence from us. It is not a punishment, though it may feel like it. He withdraws the "mountaintop" feeling because He wants us to get to work on developing the character of Christ, which He knows will not happen as long as we are being overwhelmed with His presence. When we are on that mountaintop, we are not susceptible to temptation. As attractive as sin appears to be, it cannot compete with the supercharged sense of God being alive inside. We are not seduced by temptation when we are at His side and hearing His voice. The lure of sin is simply not strong enough. That is not because we are righteous, however. It is because He is so good.

---

[11] Romans 5:3-5

Ontological Truth

When we meet Jesus as "the way, the truth, and the life,"[12] we come to know Him as a person, and not just as a figure of history. He is alive and active. As Francis Schaffer said, "He is there, and He is not silent."[13]

We also begin to be introduced to the concept of absolute, or ontological, truth. If Jesus is "*the* truth" instead of just a theory or "*a* truth," then He forms the foundation, or at least one of the foundation stones, of our lives. This key place is where the unconverted often go astray and get seduced into a false journey and pursuit of a Jesus (or some substitute) of their own imagination. That will be dealt with in detail later. This is not to say that it is easy, especially for those beginning the journey, to discern the voice of the Spirit in their interior lives. Because it is new, it is easy to miss. Because it often speaks in surprises, it is tempting to ignore. The maturing disciple will pay close attention to listening. God, of course, is more than kind. He knows how hard it is for us to hear and, in these early times of the journey, "turns up the volume" go make it easier for us. "The Voice" will sometimes come with conviction to the beginner, but most often it will bring encouragement. God knows how fragile our hearts are.

It is comforting to learn that God loves us so much that He wants us to learn Who He really is and to learn the way of holiness. He loves us so much that, in order to lead us into that gracious future, He takes us through what we *need* to receive, rather than just giving us what we *want*. Imagine how a child who is given everything he or she wants becomes spoiled and "bratty." The same could be true spiritually, but God will not have it so. Instead, He leads us into a series of experiences to help us learn about ourselves, our gifts, our sin, and His holiness. Classically, these passages have been called "Dark Nights" because our flesh does not like them at all.

---

12 John 14:6
13 Francis A. Scaeffer, *He is There and He is Not Silent*, Tyndale House Publishers, 1980

Application

1. Thinking back to the days of *your* "mountaintop experience," how would you describe some specific ways in which your life changed? How did the new relationship with Jesus Christ affect other people in your life, especially your family members?

2. What truths became especially relevant for your life, or what teachings of your past did you need to discard as you embraced the truths you encountered in Scripture? What changes in your life did you make because of this new awareness of God's ways?

Thank you, Lord Jesus, for the revelations that You gave (and give) me. Help me to remember and cherish them as I proceed along this journey, knowing that those days were preparation and a promise to help carry me through greater changes in my life. I thank you, too, for the reality that You want me to mature and that the maturity is not defined on the mountaintop but in faithfulness along the "valleys" and "highways" of life. Thank you that no challenge can come to me that You do not allow, and that challenges are designed to make me more like You and, ultimately, to bring glory to the Father. I submit myself to the Holy Spirit's ongoing work in my life. Amen.

3. If you have just prayed the prayer at the end of Chapter One or in some other way have recently come to faith in Jesus Christ and are still enjoying the "mountaintop," what is especially meaningful to you at this time?

Thank you, Lord Jesus, for the revelation of Your presence and the joy of relationship with You. Help me to be patient with others, who are in different places on the journey and have encountered challenges I have yet to face, for they don't always demonstrate the enthusiasm I am having right now. Please remind me of these special days and of the truths regarding the journey when it is time for me to come down from the mountaintop and proceed with other steps along the spiritual journey to maturity. Amen.

CHAPTER THREE

The Active Dark Night of the Senses

Where have you hidden, Beloved,
and left me moaning?
you fled like the stag
after wounding me;
I went out calling you,
but you were gone.[14]

Staying on the Path

The first of the dark nights is the ***Active Dark Night of the Senses***. It is called *active* because we are asked to *do* something. It is *dark* because it is painful. And it is the *night of the senses* because He removes the sense of His presence. What does He want from us? He wants us to put one foot in front of another and stay on the path. He wants us to dress up and show up for work, for worship, and for doing the right thing. He is asking us to *do* something. He is asking us to grow and to learn to walk by faith. It is excruciatingly painful. Every fiber of our being wants to go back to the "happy place" on the mountaintop. We are just like Peter on the Mount of Transfiguration who babbles, "It is good that we are here, let's build three booths..."[15] and **stay!** Our flesh wants to believe the lie that it is the mountaintop for which we were

---

[14] *The Collected Works of St. John of the Cross*, Translated by Kiernan Kavanaugh, OCD, and Otilio Rodriguez, OCD, revised edition (1991). Stanzas Between the Soul and the Bridegroom.
[15] Matthew 17:4

The Spiritual Journey

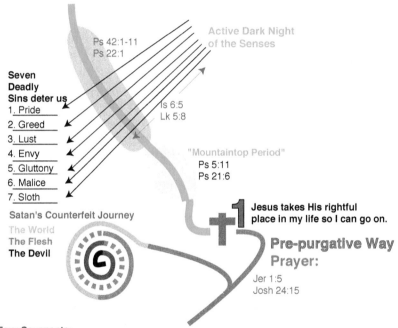

Purgative Way

Ps 42:1-11
Ps 22:1

Active Dark Night
of the Senses

**Seven
Deadly
Sins deter us**
1. Pride
2. Greed
3. Lust
4. Envy
5. Gluttony
6. Malice
7. Sloth

Is 6:5
Lk 5:8

"Mountaintop Period"
Ps 5:11
Ps 21:6

Satan's Counterfeit Journey
The World
The Flesh
The Devil

**Jesus takes His rightful
place in my life so I can go on.**

**Pre-purgative Way
Prayer:**
Jer 1:5
Josh 24:15

Four Covenants:

1. To accept God's invitation to join the journey with Jesus Christ and to be born of the Spirit.
2.
3.
4.

© Kaye Briscoe King w/ Bill Atwood

created. Having been so empty for so long, and starting to get filled with His presence and the knowledge of His love, the flesh, indulgent and immature as it is, does not want to go anywhere else. It just wants to revel in the love it is freshly experiencing.

At this point, many people become discouraged. In fact, entire denominations have emerged that are geared to simply staying on the mountaintop. They do so because they think it is the right thing to do. Their flesh cries out for it, but it is not the end of the journey, it is the beginning. It is extremely helpful when someone is there to say to us, "This is the way," and to remind us that God loves us. It is very encouraging to know that it is fully in God's plan to help us to grow by withdrawing the sense of His presence:

> In this you greatly rejoice, though now for a little while, if need be, you have been grieved by various trials, that the genuineness of your faith, *being* much more precious than gold that perishes, though it is tested by fire, may be found to praise, honor, and glory at the revelation of Jesus Christ, whom having not seen you love.[16]

Hopefully, it is encouraging to know that what is happening to us is actually *supposed to happen!* Of course, we will be glad to know that the trials will one day pass, but they must be addressed. When I first encountered the first Dark Night, with great grief I had a sense that the sin in my life had to be addressed. There had, of course, been things that I had confessed before, but this was more searching. I can remember praying, "Lord, I know that you can work swiftly with sharp pain to address things, or less painfully or dramatically over a long period of time. I just want you to know that I think it would be best to have a quick surgical move to take care of this." You can well imagine my embarrassed surprise as the words came to me, "Son, in your case there is so much to deal with it will be extremely painful over a very long time."

In this first dark night, we are also confronted with our sin in a deeper way than we have ever known before. We may a l r e a d y have had an awareness that we have sinned, but it is in this first dark night that we see the connection between *our* sin and the death of Jesus Christ. When we see Him weeping and dying for *our* sins instead of just for those of the world, the Cross takes on a totally new meaning. We begin to see sin as an obstacle and as an offence against the holiness of God. We think we are seeing it at its deepest and blackest level because that is all the insight we have. There is more to be revealed

---

[16] I Peter 1:6-8

about the true condition of our hearts, much like those little Russian dolls that have more and more dolls packed inside them. It is at this stage that God begins asking us to stop acting out our sin. We think we are "completely committed" to Him when we stop robbing grocery stores and stop punching people in the nose. The sense is that we have plumbed the depths of righteousness, and for all we know, we have. There is, however, a great deal unseen. Ultimately, God will have to work on our inner lives and motives if we are to become like Christ, but for now, He emphasizes cleaning up our behavior. Inner life and motives come later.

Seven Deadly Sins

In the Purgative Way, we begin to inventory our lives and realize that sin is an ongoing problem. If we are wise, we will allow the discovery of our particular area of vulnerability to be known. In every person's life, all of the "Seven Deadly Sins" are active in one way or another. There will be one, however, that will be a special "friend." It will, just like a puppy, follow us around and seek to get to us. For most of us, this area of sin will dog us for our entire lives. It is the entry path for evil and disobedience. Coming to recognize it, however, is very helpful. So helpful, in fact, that the church Fathers refer to the discovery as the *felix cupula (L., "the happy fault")*. That phrase may seem to be a funny name, but it is "happy" when we discover our greatest point of vulnerability. When it comes to the seductive assaults of Satan, "Forewarned is forearmed." The seven deadly sins are:

- Pride
- Greed
- Lust
- Gluttony
- Malice
- Sloth
- Envy

Pride

Pride is at the heart of almost every sin. It is the choice to say or act out, "I am better than you." Even worse, it is a rejection of the Lordship of our Creator. It is the root of the central spiritual conflict of all time. In a passage that describes judgment on the King of Babylon, we see the struggle of heaven echoed in Satan's attitude:

For you have said in your heart:
"I will ascend into heaven,
I will exalt my throne above the stars of God;
I will also sit on the mount of the congregation
On the farthest sides of the north;
I will ascend above the heights of the clouds,
I will be like the Most High."
Yet you shall be brought down to Sheol,
To the lowest depths of the Pit.[17]

Both the heart of pride and its consequence are found in those verses. We desire to be God, to have things *our* way, and when we act that out, the consequence is terrible. George Bernard Shaw observed, "There are true great truths: There is a God, and you are not He." He also said, "It is amazing that the one doctrine (original sin) so readily observable, is paid so little attention."

Pride causes us to choose shortcuts, rationalize ungodly behavior, and disregard Scripture and propriety. It should come as no surprise that it creates great problems.

Greed

It is easy to see how pride is woven into greedy decisions. Greed is the imbalance of taking that which is not our own, and it naturally rises out of listening to that inner voice calling us into indulgence. Along with the act is the assumption that we "deserve" what we want, and it involves always wanting more than we have, which means we are never satisfied. This is why Jesus warned,

> "Do not lay up for yourselves treasures on earth, where moth and rust destroy and where thieves break in and steal; but lay up for yourselves treasure in heaven, where neither moth nor rust destroys and where thieves do not break in and steal. For where your treasure is, there your heart will be also."[18]

Greed, like much other sin, is easy to rationalize because the process that leads up to acting out is an interior one. It is only when it is ready to bear fruit that it can be seen. Add to that the fact that people often have skewed perceptions. When greedy acts are perpetrated, the offender often sees the acts as "just what they need to do in order to get their due."

---

[17] Isaiah 14:13-15
[18] Matthew 6:19-21

Lust

As can readily be seen with other of the "Seven Deadlies," this cardinal sin starts with a virtue whose boundaries are transgressed. The Anglican scholar who served as Bishop of Durham, Tom Wright, observed at a lecture in Oxford, "Fire is good in the fireplace."[19] Lust does not just refer to sexual license. It can impact other areas of life, but far too often, it powerfully involves misuse of sexual identity. One of the most insidious aspects of lust is that it is not only involved in sexual acts themselves, but the psychological grip extends toward compulsively controlling the person's thoughts. In addition, just as greed is all but impossible to satisfy, the lust of the flesh when fully embraced becomes harder and harder to satiate. The distortions of Western culture greatly exacerbate the problem as well. When the population is inundated with sexual messages, it is inevitable that some people will be seduced to get started on a distorted path. Tragically, the Church has been miserable at offering positive teaching on marriage and sexuality.

At the General Convention of the Episcopal Church in Indianapolis in 1994 during a debate on human sexuality, Jay Walker, the Bishop of Long Island (NY) said, "If you are suggesting that having sex is only within the context of marriage, that just won't fly in my diocese." With such leadership in the church, is it any wonder that our culture is lost in a sexual wilderness?

How different that attitude is from the admonition found in I John 2:15 and following:

> Do not love the world or the things in the world. If anyone loves the world, the love of the Father is not in him. For all that is in the world – the lust of the flesh, the lust of the eyes, and the pride of life – is not of the Father but is of the world. And the world is passing away, and the lust of it; but he who does the will of God abides forever.

Gluttony

Although gluttony obviously involves healthy and temperate limits of consumption of food and drink, it can involve much more. Woven together closely with greed and lust, gluttony can involve the intemperate pursuit or consumption of *anything* physical, not just food and drink. It is not hard to make a case that this is an area of sin that rises out of wounds in one's life, but that argument can often be made for any sin. Gluttony requires a special kind of grace to overcome because, unlike some of its sister sins, it is not possible to completely forgo food or drink. One can choose accountability to avoid sexual

---

[19] Tom (N.T.) Wright, "Lecture," Oxford, 2002

misconduct or the embrace of malice, but eliminating food is impossible. When healthy and appropriate boundaries are not in place, many who are caught up in this "deadly" sin seem to be too overwhelmed to set limits. Gluttony also has a particularly sharp edge in that it twins excess behavior and self-loathing in the classic cycle of addiction associated with alcoholism. Much self-discipline is needed, which perhaps is why Paul in writing to the church at Corinth encouraged them with these words:

> Do you not know that those who run in a race all run, but one receives the prize? Run in such a way that you may obtain it. And everyone who competes *for the prize* is temperate in all things. Now they *do it* to obtain a perishable crown, but we *for* an imperishable *crown*.[20]

Malice

Malice is a prideful, self-centered, indulgent hatred. The open door to begin this deadly sin often is injustice. It may even be great injustice. Hurt and anger are not the problem, however. The nurturing of the offense and the replay of mental images of revenge are what pollute one's heart. The author of Hebrews speaks about the defilement that can set in and damage an entire community.

> Follow peace with all *men*, and holiness, without which no man shall see the Lord: Looking diligently lest any man fail of the grace of God; lest any root of bitterness springing up trouble *you*, and thereby many be defiled.[21]

Malice is like a spiritual malignancy that grows and grows and grows. Without intervention, it can bring grief to many. At its heart, pride is also active. It is the delusion that community norms do not apply to one's self (for whatever reason). The person motivated by malice comes to believe that it is his or her "right" to exact revenge. At its most perverse, people can become so distorted that they act hatefully when there is not even an excuse to do so.

Sloth

Classically understood as laziness, there is much more to sloth than that. It can be as simple as being lazy about doing the things that are important, but it can be more subtle. A slothful person might be extremely energetic at a hobby but simply "forget" to provide for the family, or be very work-oriented but fail to give attention to one's personal

---

[20] I Corinthians 9:24-25
[21] Hebrews 12:14-15

hygiene or to the family's emotional needs. It can even affect relationships. For example, sometimes people think the besetting sin in an inappropriate sexual relationship is lust, when it is actually sloth that refuses to invest the energy required to make a commitment to and nurture an appropriate marriage relationship. Instead, the slothful approach mimics the intimacies of marriage when there is no foundation for them.

Envy

Envy is like an itch that can't be reached inside a cast. It is maddening because it cannot be satisfied. There will always be someone who has something you don't. Whether it is material possessions, a position, or a gift or talent, for the envious individual, it is painfully desired. There is no sense of celebration for other people's graces; rather there is only a pathological drive to have whatever is desired. James described the dire consequences of envy:

> For where envy and self-seeking exit, confusion and every evil
> thing are there.[22]

Sometimes envy is born of lack, but there are many poor people who are generous. Envy has to do with an exaggerated sense of importance about who we are and a prideful, slothful, even malicious disregard for the condition, circumstance, or welfare of others. All that those caught in the grip of envy can see is what they do *not* have. Once acquired, it quickly loses its luster and is often forgotten, but probably not discarded.

In the first of the dark nights, the Active Dark Night of the Senses, we lose the sense that God is with us because we don't feel His presence. At the same time, the journey provides the opportunity to identify and begin to deal with our besetting sin.

There is a spiritual way to do that, however.

Prayer-Life Elocutions

As we begin to develop a sense of gratitude for what God has done for us, it is possible to have hearts of thanksgiving, even when we are not fresh in the blush of the supernatural revelation of His love like it was when we reached the first mountaintop. It is natural for us to begin to shape prayers that rise from our hearts. It is at this stage that

---

[22] James 3:16

"elocutions" rise. Elocutions are prayers that we shape ourselves. Literally meaning "good speech," these "good prayers" are not the finely crafted theological statements of the historic liturgies of the Church, but they are heartfelt, and without question, it pleases God that we begin forming them. We are meant to mature and grow in our prayer life, and this is the second step. In a way, it is the most important step of prayer because it is the first o n e that is consciously our own.

Most people find that beginning to pray is an awkward situation. This feeling of awkwardness may result from their experiences of prayer being largely limited to liturgical prayer, and they wonder, "How can I be expected to pray like the Book of Common Prayer or the Westminster Catechism?" Or, they may come from a faith tradition that features primarily a "rote" form of prayer that sounds "pietistic" but is not sincerely from the heart. They wonder, "How can I pray in my own words, without the formulated phrases that are sprinkled throughout what I am use to hearing?" In all cases, the answer is: I can't, at least not yet, but I can begin to pray sincere prayers that rise from my heart and life experience. There are two factors that can help overcome this hesitancy dramatically. The *first* is to pray out loud, even when alone. There is something powerful about prayers spoken aloud. The *second* suggestion is to find someone else with whom to pray even simple prayers. To begin with, they may be prayers of only three words: "God Bless Mom," but that will quickly grow. The important matter is to *start* praying. The Holy Spirit will direct and increase our prayer lives once we take the initial step.

Application
Discerning Besetting Sin

1. Everyone is assaulted by sin and can be hampered by any of the "seven deadly sins." There is, however, usually one area that the devil uses over and over to mount his attacks on our lives. Coming to know this area of assault forewarns us and can help us have a much more victorious life. Which of the seven deadly sins represents the area in which you experience the most difficulty? What specific steps or actions can you take – or what decisions can you make – to thwart the enemy's attempts to defeat you in this area?

2. Coming to know our "besetting sin" is helpful and gives us a strategic insight in victoriously battling the devil. For this reason, it is sometimes called the *"Felix Cupula,"* Latin for "Happy Fault." How might your life be different now if you can be forewarned of the devil's attacks?

3. Sometimes the attacks are so intense that we need help from someone else. It is important that this person be someone we can trust and who will keep confidences. Do you have anyone (a close friend or relative, priest, pastor, spiritual director) who can help you when you are attacked or to whom you give accountability? If so, what counsel has that person offered? How well are you following it?

Heavenly Father, thank you for loving me despite all my shortcomings. I confess my besetting sin of _____. I ask You to forgive me for each instance when I have given in to this sin. I claim Your forgiveness and my position in Jesus Christ, which gives me victory, through the Spirit's empowerment, over this sin. I yield myself to the Holy Spirit's work to reveal the areas that I need to address and the measures I need to take in order to stand against the enemy's attacks. Thank you for your desire that I become more like Jesus, even though dealing with some of these issues is really difficult sometimes! Amen.

CHAPTER FOUR

The "Peaceful Meadow"

Once momentum is firmly established in our lives and we have demonstrated that we are committed to moving along on the journey, there is no need for the sharp pain of the Active Dark Night of the Senses to continue. Although it may last for years in some people's lives, it is like a butterfly's chrysalis from which an extraordinarily beautiful butterfly emerges. From the moment the dark night begins, God's design is that we should emerge from it with a new beauty. That next place in the journey is sometimes called a *"Peaceful Meadow."* As the sense of God's presence begins to return, it opens an even deeper place of peace in our lives. The psalmist expresses it this way:

> He shall come down like rain upon the grass before mowing,
> Like showers *that* water the earth.
> In His days the righteous shall flourish,
> And abundance of peace.[23]

The Active Dark Night of the Senses has done its work when we become convinced that our commitment to Christ has seriously marked our lives. It is becoming indelible. We are becoming known for being followers of Jesus. Now, the work must proceed for us to become more and more like Him. The process will continue until we fully manifest the measure of the stature of the fullness of Christ in our lives.[24] There will be time enough for challenge later, after a respite, though.

---

[23] Psalm 72;6-7
[24] Ephesians 4:13

The Spiritual Journey

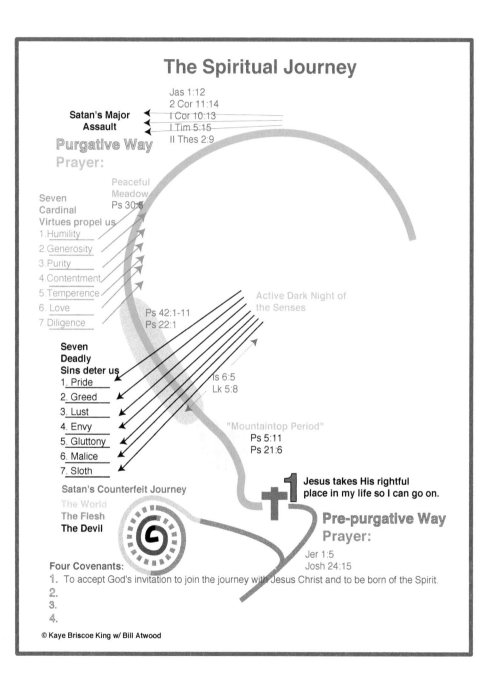

Satan's Major Assault

Jas 1:12
2 Cor 11:14
I Cor 10:13
I Tim 5:15
II Thes 2:9

Purgative Way
Prayer:

Peaceful Meadow
Ps 30:5

Seven Cardinal Virtues propel us
1. Humility
2. Generosity
3. Purity
4. Contentment
5. Temperence
6. Love
7. Diligence

Ps 42:1-11
Ps 22:1

Active Dark Night of the Senses

Seven Deadly Sins deter us
1. Pride
2. Greed
3. Lust
4. Envy
5. Gluttony
6. Malice
7. Sloth

Is 6:5
Lk 5:8

"Mountaintop Period"
Ps 5:11
Ps 21:6

Satan's Counterfeit Journey
The World
The Flesh
The Devil

Jesus takes His rightful place in my life so I can go on.

Pre-purgative Way
Prayer:

Jer 1:5
Josh 24:15

Four Covenants:
1. To accept God's invitation to join the journey with Jesus Christ and to be born of the Spirit.
2.
3.
4.

© Kaye Briscoe King w/ Bill Atwood

God graciously gives us a gift of peace when we need it, a chance to catch our breath and still our hearts. One of the particularly sweet things about the peaceful meadow is that we again experience the presence of God that we missed so much during the first dark night. It is also a time when God begins working to develop changes in our attitudes and behaviors that reveal our new relationship with Him. These new attitudes are sometimes called "cardinal virtues."

Cultivating Virtues

Rather than combating the Seven Deadly Sins by gritting our teeth and saying, "I will not do 'xyz' anymore," there is another way to do battle with sin. It is in the cultivation of the Cardinal Virtues. For each area of sin, there is an attendant virtue that can be cultivated. The fruit of that cultivation is spiritual strength that can help subdue the call of the flesh.
   The Cardinal Virtues are twinned with the sins:

Pride	Humility
Greed	Generosity
Lust	Chastity (Purity)
Gluttony	Temperance
Malice	Love (Charity)
Sloth	Industry (Diligence)
Envy	Contentment

The Virtues propel us toward holiness. The beauty of virtues is that they involve behaviors that can be chosen. We can choose a humble seat, take the small piece of cake, share resources with others, and commit to fidelity of relationship. We can choose temperance, choose to forgive, actively pursue godliness, and practice contentment. It will be a great strain initially, but eventually, those choices will begin to bear the fruit of the Spirit and it will become easier as we develop a new nature that is more like Christ. If we don't know what is possible or appropriate, it is unlikely that we will choose it. For that reason, conversation with others about the journey is very valuable to us as we begin our spiritual journey in earnest.

Humility
Pride is undone by humility. By participating in it, we are walking in the footsteps of Jesus and embracing the way of the cross:

> Let this mind be in you which was also in Christ Jesus, who, being in the form of God, did not consider it robbery to be equal with God, but made Himself of no reputation, taking the form of a bondservant, and coming in the likeness of men. And being found in appearance as a man, He humbled Himself and became obedient to the point of death, even the death of the cross.[25]

There is something about the flesh that cries out to be exalted, not subdued. Despite this inclination, the exaltation of the flesh is not satisfying, whereas walking humbly is. As we choose the lesser seat, turn attention away from ourselves, or work quietly at mundane tasks of service, the character of Christ is rising in us. Its fruits are usually evident to others around us who are close to us, long before we see a change, but the fruits will certainly come.

Generosity

The call to walk with generosity does not mean that we have to divest ourselves of all our possessions; rather, it means that we should live with something of the lavish generosity with which Jesus has treated us. When, in human terms, circumstances call for a response, the Spirit suggests a lavish one. Rather than assuming that we buy something new and give away the old, the Lord may prod us to make do with the old and give the new away. It is not the way that we tend to think naturally. Left to our own devices, the natural man believes that we are at the center of the universe. Generosity nudges us from that throne by asking that we share of our substance, not just out of abundance, and that we do so with generosity, for "God loves a cheerful giver."[26]

Chastity (Purity)

History has demonstrated that any arena of human endeavor can be distorted. The virtue of purity calls us to reverse that situation and make choices that are in agreement with God's design. Sexuality expressed chastely in marriage, resources prayerfully applied, language and relationships that reflect the gentle grace of Jesus are all examples of purity. We are all too familiar with the tug toward the titillating and even perverse, but purity calls us to say "no" to that and "yes" to the path of life. It isn't that we don't know what is pure; rather, it is that we too readily cave in to the flesh. Purity calls us *not* to do so; it challenges us *not* to give into the world. Paul gives wise advise on how to make that choice:

---

[25] Philippians 2:5-8
[26] II Corinthians 9:7

> I beseech you therefore, brethren, by the mercies of God, that you present your bodies a living sacrifice, holy, acceptable to God, which is your reasonable service. And do not be conformed to this world, but be transformed by the renewing of your mind, that you may prove what is that good and acceptable and perfect will of God. . . . Abhor what is evil. Cling to what is good.[27]

Temperance

Just as is the case with the seven deadly sins, the cardinal virtues are woven together with a great deal of overlap. So it is with temperance. It is partly about contentment and simplicity. Mostly it is *choosing* propriety in food, drink, money, sexuality, and even life itself:

> Let us walk properly, as in the day, not in revelry and drunkenness, not in lewdness and lust, not in strife and envy. But put on the Lord Jesus Christ, and make no provision for the flesh, to fulfill its lusts.[28]

Love (Charity)

Love is relatively simple to cultivate, yet it is surprising that it is often so painful to do so. We would like to think of love always being accompanied by the fluttering feeling in our hearts that bubbles with joy. In reality, whereas the recipient experiences gracefulness, blessing, and joy, the lover has often paid a price. Love is not so much a feeling as it is an action. Where love is genuine, the price is gladly paid, but it can be very costly. In Jesus' case, it cost Him everything. In ours, He says, "Greater love has no one than this, than to lay down one's life for his friends."[29] When we begin to live that way, we are manifesting the life and ministry of Jesus and will, inevitably, become more like Him.

Industry (Diligence)

The Spirit's assault on sloth is the apparently uninspiring pursuit of diligence. It is closely associated with perseverance. To keep going when we are tired or discouraged takes discipline. Many of us have lived with such rebellion that we easily fall prey to the voice that says, "*mañana* -- I'll do it tomorrow or not at all!" Bit by bit, diligence unglues sloth until a new reality emerges, and perseverance leads to maturity and completeness, such that we lack nothing.[30]

---

[27] Romans 12:1-2,9
[28] Romans 13:13-14.
[29] John 15:13
[30] James 1:4

Contentment

It is particularly difficult for American Christians, who live with abundance and the bombardment of advertising that demands more and more "stuff," to realize that we have "enough." The seduction is subtle that causes our desires to gravitate not to the least common denominator of possessions, wealth, or conditions, but to the most extravagant. It causes us to forget that

> . . . godliness with contentment is great gain. For we brought nothing into this world, *and it is* certain we can carry nothing out. And having food and clothing, with these we shall be content. But those who desire to be rich fall into temptation and a snare, and *into* many foolish and harmful lusts which drown men in destruction and perdition. For the love of money is a root of all *kinds of* evil, for which some have strayed from the faith in their greediness, and pierced themselves through with many sorrows.[31]

Contentment says, "This is enough!" or even, "With so much, surely I can share." The flesh complains with the precise prosecution of a skilled debater, but the cultivation of contentment can make us more like Jesus, who reminds us that where our treasure is, there will our heart be also.

As we walk in the purgative way, we should begin pursuing these virtues. The most critical of them to pursue will, of course, be the virtue that is twinned with our besetting sin. It is our best hope for a peaceful and fruitful Christian life.

Satan's Major Assault

As we catch our breath in this peaceful meadow, two things will be happening. It is obvious that Satan does not want us to be where we are or where we are going. He will prepare to launch a major assault to derail our deepening commitment. After we have been only a short time in the meadow, he will initiate his evil attack, with the hope of leading us astray. This assault is remarkably sophisticated. It will attempt to exploit our besetting sins and areas of vulnerability. Peter warns us that we must "be sober [and] vigilant; because [our] enemy the devil walks about like a roaring lion, seeking whom he may devour."[32]

Whatever shape a temptation might take to be most enticing, it is almost assured to present itself. The Enemy knows that if we pass this point, it is exceedingly unlikely that we will turn away from Christ.

---

[31] I Timothy 6:6-10
[32] I Peter 5:8

Though we may walk in circles for a while or even stall or slip a bit, we are on the verge of experiencing Jesus in a way that is utterly captivating. Sin is certainly possible, but we will come to see the illumination of our lives with the Holy Spirit in a way that is deeply fulfilling.

It is not that we are flawless in our relationship or even our walk with Him. What happens is that we become indelibly committed to Him and to the journey. Whether it is possible for someone who has come to faith to be lost to perdition after conversion is a subject of a great deal of theological debate. It is obviously the case that there are people who, even if they will ultimately be with God in heaven, are leading lives that tragically are not victorious. We do not need to concern ourselves with that issue at this point.

As we process the devil's assault, remembering what we have learned from the first Dark Night, and ponder the loveliness of Christ, we find that we have an increased desire to move forward on the journey. We recognize, however, that there is more to this journey than we first thought. In fact, there is a stark realization: *we cannot do this on our own*!

We cry out to God in a *second covenant*. It is the realization of twelve-step programs and the Christian life in general that we need something more than we have in ourselves to continue, to prosper, and to fulfill our Christian calling. This second covenant involves entering into a dependency similar to that of the first covenant. In the first covenant, we realized that we cannot save ourselves; now, we come to the humble realization that we cannot continue the journey and get to the place we need to go without God's help.

Shortly after this point, we move into the next season of our journey: *The Illuminative Way*. It is so called because our way is being illuminated by the Holy Spirit. It captivates and overwhelms anything else we have known thus far. We just desire to be with Him in the power of the Spirit.

> Now I occupy my soul
> and all my energy in his service;
> I no longer tend the herd,
> nor have I any other work
> now that my every act is love.[33]

---

[33] *Collected Works*, Stanzas Between the Soul and the Bridegroom, Stanza 28

Application
Cultivating Virtues

1. Rather than battling against sin directly, the Kingdom model is to overwhelm evil with good. Instead of gritting your teeth and vowing to "do better" in battling your besetting sin, a better approach is to cultivate the attendant virtue. In the list below of the Seven Deadly Sins, you can see the attendant Cardinal Virtue:

Pride	Humility
Greed	Generosity
Lust	Chastity (Purity)
Gluttony	Temperance
Malice	Love (Charity)
Sloth	Industry (Diligence)
Envy	Contentment

What is the attending Virtue to the cardinal sin you identified earlier?

2. How would your behavior be different if you were to pursue the appropriate Virtue instead of succumbing to your besetting sin?

3. Your victory over the sin will not happen over night, but it *will* begin when you choose to take a first stop. What will be your first step, *today*?

You can pray,

Lord, help me develop the virtue of _____ so that I can be more conformed to Your character.

SECTION THREE

THE ILLUMINATIVE WAY

CHAPTER FIVE

The Spirit of God – The Illuminative Way

In this new portion of the journey, we come to know the Spirit, to follow His lead, to learn of His gifts, and to experience His power. One of the great hallmarks of the *Illuminative Way* is that people begin to think of the Holy Spirit as a "person" ("He" rather than "it"). Intimacy with the Spirit is essential to opening one's life to the transformation that is possible in Christ. This is a season of great growth and fruitful ministry. There are some indications that it was only in the Illuminative Way that people were released into ministry in the early churches. How different the situation is today! Many clergy today are still in the pre-purgative way.

Supernatural Work of the Spirit

It is always a mistake to compare one Christian with another. We all are different, and our circumstances are different. It is not illegitimate, however, to ask if a given Christian is moving to fulfill his or her potential in Christ. Although there are many subtleties in approaches to the Christian journey, some are not subtle at all. When people first come to faith in Christ, they set off on the Purgative Way to follow Him. Many people are deeply committed and willing to do everything in their power to be faithful to His call. Some people, however, will take another step and say, "Lord I am committed to following You, *and* I open my life to You for You to work as you choose, naturally or supernaturally."

The openness for God to work supernaturally is a key point of submission. It opens our lives to a whole new range of miracles, gifts, and abundance of fruit. The point is not whether one Christian is more fruitful than another. The question is whether or not we are moving

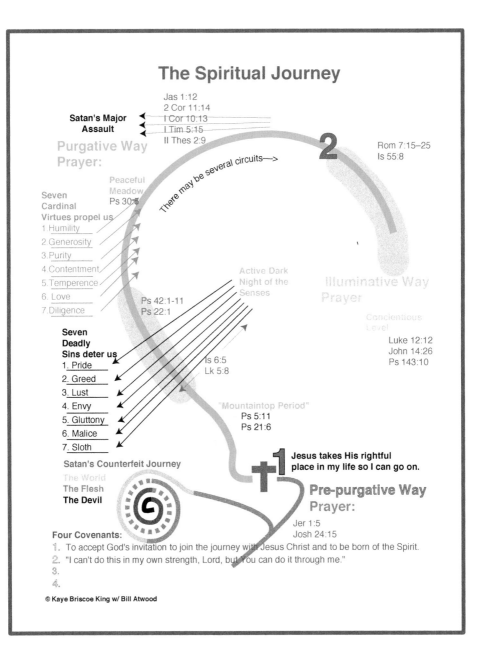

The Spiritual Journey

Jas 1:12
2 Cor 11:14
Satan's Major Assault — I Cor 10:13
I Tim 5:15
II Thes 2:9

Rom 7:15–25
Is 55:8

Purgative Way Prayer:

There may be several circuits →

Peaceful Meadow
Ps 30:5

Seven Cardinal Virtues propel us
1. Humility
2. Generosity
3. Purity
4. Contentment
5. Temperence
6. Love
7. Diligence

Ps 42:1-11
Ps 22:1

Active Dark Night of the Senses

Illuminative Way Prayer

Concientious Level
Luke 12:12
John 14:26
Ps 143:10

Seven Deadly Sins deter us
1. Pride
2. Greed
3. Lust
4. Envy
5. Gluttony
6. Malice
7. Sloth

Is 6:5
Lk 5:8

Satan's Counterfeit Journey
The World
The Flesh
The Devil

"Mountaintop Period"
Ps 5:11
Ps 21:6

Jesus takes His rightful place in my life so I can go on.

Pre-purgative Way Prayer:
Jer 1:5
Josh 24:15

Four Covenants:
1. To accept God's invitation to join the journey with Jesus Christ and to be born of the Spirit.
2. "I can't do this in my own strength, Lord, but You can do it through me."
3.
4.

© Kaye Briscoe King w/ Bill Atwood

toward fulfilling our potential. Without question, every Christian who is open to God to work supernaturally will bear more fruit than the same person would bear if he or she were not open to the flow of the Spirit.

Because God chooses to be gentle and gracious with us, He does not force those who are not open to miraculous gifts to manifest them. Without our "permission," God will allow us to live below our potential and not manifest what is possible. It may be as simple as saying that an evangelist who is open to the supernatural work of the Spirit will bear more fruit than when he is not open. Letting God set the limits means that we can manifest pneumatic (or charismatic) gifts as the Spirit wills.[34]

The Holy Spirit and Discernment

There is another issue of maturity that becomes clearer in the Illuminative Way. It has to do with discerning more subtle direction from the Holy Spirit. When we are first converted, most of the demands of obedience are external. God asks us to stop overtly breaking Commandments and bring our behavior in line with the lifestyle of the Kingdom. As we move into the Illuminative Way, we find the demands become greater and deeper. We are dramatically confronted with two changes:

Cleansing our Interior Lives
First of all, we are asked to begin to bring our interior lives in line with the Kingdom. God challenges our *interior* lives. It may appear to an outside observer that we are righteous, but God is unimpressed with our outward appearance if our hearts are corrupt. We are reminded of God's caution to Samuel:

> For the Lord does not see as man sees; for man looks at the outward appearance, but the Lord looks at the heart.[35]

In the Illuminative Way, we are called to work on bringing our attitudes and hearts in line with the principles of Jesus. It is a very challenging time. Later in the Illuminative Way, in what is called the *"conscientious way,"* God really turns up the heat to reveal every mixed motive and hypocritical act. He is not doing that to inflict pain on our lives (though it certainly does!); rather, He does it to help us shed the drain of "the flesh" so we can be prepared to spend eternity in union with Him.

---

[34] I Corinthians 12:11
[35] I Samuel 16:7b

Discernment and Obedience

Second, there is another change: discernment. The Christian life is a series of apparent contradictions:

> Justice and Mercy
> Stillness and Activity
> Work and Prayer
> Confident Intimacy and Awesome Inscrutability

It is not that any of these things is "wrong"; instead, we must hear and respond to the voice of the Spirit to know which is the right and spiritually lively thing for *right now.* Something that is inherently good but ill-timed can do a great deal of damage. Should I challenge a friend or let his or her wound go? Should a child be disciplined or cuddled this time? Should we worship with the exuberance of Psalm 150 or fall silent on our knees? We must learn not only the right *thing*, but also the right *way* and the right *time.* Faithfulness can demand no other course. Those who never grapple with the subtleties of the Spirit are doomed to make wrong choices far too often.

It is not accurate to say that our choices always should make sense. In fact, sometimes the Spirit calls for actions that do *not* make sense – humanly. One example occurred on February 16, 1977, when Archbishop Jonani Luwum of Uganda told his House of Bishops that he was going to confront Idi Amin, Uganda's cruel dictator. They objected and told him that he would be killed. "Of course," replied Luwum. The Spirit had called him to bear witness, even though it cost him his life. As a result, the fruits of faith in Uganda were greatly enhanced. To some people, it was a needless waste, but the fruit bears witness that his act bore the Spirit's blessing.

In our lives, we face simpler challenges, but they are important nonetheless. In the Illuminative Way, we learn how to listen and walk faithfully with the Spirit.

A Thirst for the Word

In the Illuminative Way, there is also a fresh kindling of interest in the Scriptures. This time, it is not a desire for information so much as it is a search for life. In the Illuminative Way, people will often spend many hours or days with the Lord in His Word. Along with this interest is a new kind of revelatory prayer called *meditation.* Meditative prayer is focusing on a passage of Scripture, hoping and praying that God will reveal something about Himself and His Kingdom in it. It is a specific longing and yearning that we connect and learn from Him. It is at this point that the promise begins to be true that we "have no need of a teacher, for it is the Holy Spirit who will teach."[36] It would be silly to say that a new convert does not need any instruction, but a person in the Illuminative Way can abundantly learn directly from the Holy Spirit.

Although "charismatic" word gifts may have been manifest in a person's life before this point, new insights and concepts will begin to be quickened for us. It is literally true that God the Holy Spirit illuminates the Scriptures for us so we can learn of Him. Sometimes it is very dramatic as we learn to walk in this new way. The Spirit can orchestrate our steps, ministries, and lives in very specific ways. When He does, the fruit is abundant.

It is now that the pilgrim begins to understand about Jesus as the "living Word." He is "living and powerful and sharper than any two-edged sword."[37] This becomes vital as we begin to mature and learn to apply the scriptures for guidance. He is "...piercing even to the division of soul and spirit, and of joints and marrow, and is a discerner of the thoughts and intents of the heart."[38] It is now that the finer points of discernment begin to be learned to discover what the truly spiritual choice is among the range of possibilities.

Application
The Power of the Holy Spirit

No of us can come to Christ without the work of the Holy Spirit drawing us first. It is possible, though, for a person who has become a believer to expect and plan to live in his or her own strength. Are you willing to pray to ask the Lord to strengthen you supernaturally? If so, you can pray a prayer like this:

Lord Jesus Christ, thank you for giving me new life in God's Kingdom. On my own, I do not have enough strength to live up to the full extent of what You call me to do. Please fill me with the presence and power of the Holy Spirit. You are free to use me as you will, both naturally and supernaturally. Give me strength to overcome evil, extend the grace of the Kingdom of God to others, and produce the fruit of the Holy Spirit in my life. Amen.

---

[36] I John 2:27
[37] Hebrews 4:12
[38] Ibid

CHAPTER SIX

Dark Nights of the Senses and the Spirit

The Passive Dark Night of the Senses

As we enter into the Illuminative Way, we begin to experience another "night." This one is called "passive," however, because it is not dependent on what *we* do; rather it depends on what God does as He is at work in us. Not only does progress rely on Him, but also whatever fruit appears is manifest because of His grace, not because of our efforts or energy.

Most of the time, the person who is traversing the ***Passive Dark Night of the Senses*** is blissfully unaware of the fruit that is emerging from God's work. Others can see it, though. It is not unusual for people in this portion of the journey to be told, "That was amazing! It was the best class (Bible Study/sermon/article, etc.) I've ever had!" People in the Passive Dark Night usually reply with something like, "Huh?" It's not that they are being overly modest – they really can't see it.

God's purpose for us in the Passive Dark Night is to advance our position in Him to display more and more of His grace. It is preparation for later stages when we will seek to disappear and have only Jesus be the person of focus. It involves the realization that "He must increase, but I must decrease."[39] As pilgrims proceed in the Illuminative Way, they are increasingly fruitful in what is called the *conscientious path*. It is as though they become conduits open increasingly more widely to the flow of the Holy Spirit. Prayer life changes yet again, to draw more and learn more from meditation. Time spent with the Lord yields dramatic insights

---

[39] John 3:30

The Spiritual Journey

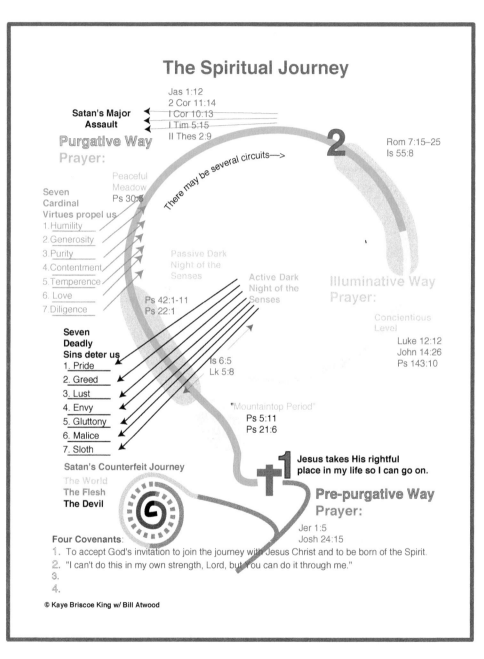

Jas 1:12
2 Cor 11:14
Satan's Major ◄ I Cor 10:13
Assault ◄ I Tim 5:15
◄ II Thes 2:9

Purgative Way
Prayer:

Peaceful
Meadow
Seven Ps 30:5
Cardinal
Virtues propel us
1. Humility
2. Generosity
3. Purity
4. Contentment
5. Temperence
6. Love
7. Diligence

There may be several circuits—>

2

Rom 7:15–25
Is 55:8

Passive Dark
Night of the
Senses

Active Dark
Night of the
Senses

Illuminative Way
Prayer:

Ps 42:1-11
Ps 22:1

Concientious
Level

Luke 12:12
John 14:26
Ps 143:10

Seven
Deadly
Sins deter us
1. Pride
2. Greed Is 6:5
3. Lust Lk 5:8
4. Envy
5. Gluttony
6. Malice
7. Sloth

"Mountaintop Period"
Ps 5:11
Ps 21:6

+1 Jesus takes His rightful
place in my life so I can go on.

Satan's Counterfeit Journey
The World
The Flesh
The Devil

Pre-purgative Way
Prayer:

Jer 1:5
Four Covenants: Josh 24:15
1. To accept God's invitation to join the journey with Jesus Christ and to be born of the Spirit.
2. "I can't do this in my own strength, Lord, but You can do it through me."
3.
4.

© Kaye Briscoe King w/ Bill Atwood

that can be life-changing.

Well into the Illuminative Way, usually after something like five decades of life, the Holy Spirit begins to prepare us for the deepest levels of intimacy and union with Christ. Naturally, fellowship begins when we are converted to Christ. That is often called *justification*, but there is an ongoing process of becoming increasingly like Jesus that is called *sanctification*. Even though God is willing to treat a person "just-as-if-I'd" never sinned, there is a need for us to be more closely conformed to Christ. The normal pattern for this process of being conformed to the image of Christ involves several inter-related and repeated processes of crucifying of the flesh, but it also involves the "stilling of the intellect," spiritual betrothal, and spiritual marriage to fulfill our capacity in Christ. That means that we cooperate in a *third covenant*, entering into the process of "crucifying the flesh"; in doing so, we learn to trust what God says as the determination of direction in our lives rather than deciding for ourselves.

Stilling of the Intellect

The process called *stilling of the intellect* does not mean that we cease to think at all. Instead, it means we don't rely on our own thoughts as supreme. Jesus leads us through a process of learning to trust His gentle leading rather than our own rational process. If this is even suggested too early in the journey, it is all but completely misunderstood.

It does not mean that we become mind-numbed robots of Jesus or other leaders; it simply means that those who are maturing in Kingdom values will find things reasonable "in Christ," that are outrageous when looked at purely intellectually. Concepts like sacrifice, integrity, and unconditional love (which are mainstays of the Kingdom of God) seem unreasonable to the "natural man." In this process, we become acutely aware of the difference between our way of doing things, and God's way, as He revealed to Isaiah:

> "For My thoughts are not your thoughts
> Nor are your ways My ways," says the Lord.
> "For as the heavens are higher than the earth,
> So are My ways higher than your ways,
> And My thoughts than your thoughts."[40]

As a result of the Fall, our fellowship with Him was devastated. It was not just that sin introduced physical death; rather, our souls, intellects, and spirits were also affected. Some scientist reckoned that we use only 10% of our intellectual capacity (during certain seasons of our life, it can be a lot less than that!). Imagine what it must have been like

---

[40] Isaiah 55:8-9

in God's original design. The Cross, of course, is His mechanism to give back to us that which we forfeited because of sin.

Throughout the journey, God is preparing us to spend eternity with Him in heaven. There is an old Yiddish expression that says visitors to your home, like fish, begin to be rank after three days. Imagine the work that God must do in our hearts to prepare us to "dwell in the house of the Lord forever."[41]

A great work is being done in the dark nights. During the Passive Dark Night of the Senses, our flesh is being crucified in ways that we could never have imagined. The pain of our sin is all but unbearable. St. John of the Cross turned to his sketch pad to show the horror of the cost of sin and the brutality of the crucifixion. His pen and ink drawing is one of the most stark portrayals of the pain of sin, both for Jesus and for our flesh as it is nailed to the cross. Today, of course, Mel Gibson's film, *The Passion of the Christ*, has given millions of people a window into the cost.

Notice in the drawing below, John looks at the Cross from the Father's perspective. Because John understood the unity that is found in the Holy Trinity, he shows the anguish on the face of the Son, turned so it is fully revealed to the Father. Because God is both three and one, it is important to remember that it is not an angry God arbitrarily sending His Son to death, but the heart of the Father is pierced at the same time as the body of Jesus is nailed to the wood of the cross. The sweat, blood and gaunt frame demonstrate something of the horror and wickedness of the way Jesus died on our behalf.

Calming of the Emotional Roller Coaster
As we mature and the journey continues, the Holy Spirit is eager to lead us away from the tyranny of our emotions. To the person on an earlier portion of the journey, this calming seems strange and undesirable. Why would the strength of feelings be a problem? After all, most of us have been held captive to them for most of our lives. Now, however, in the Illuminative Way, God wants us to learn to walk by faith, not by sight,[42] and certainly not by feelings. He is leading us to mitigate the emotional highs we have experienced before and to moderate the lows. It is as though he is saying:

> The voice of one crying in the wilderness:
> "Prepare the way of the LORD;
> Make straight in the desert
> A highway for our God.
> Every valley shall be exalted
> And every mountain and hill brought low;
> The crooked places shall be made straight
> And the rough places smooth;
> The glory of the LORD shall be revealed,
> And all flesh shall see *it* together;
> For the mouth of the LORD has spoken."[43]

This happens not by denying our feelings but rather by embracing His insights about the true nature of the value of things. We learn to love what God loves and rely less and less on circumstances. When we have heard the King of Kings give a word of blessing, the transient pains of daily life do not hold sway over us. This is one of the great works of the Illuminative Way, to begin drawing satisfaction in our hearts not from surrounding circumstances, but from the truth of God's description of our lives.

Active Dark Night of the Spirit

As the Christian pilgrim progresses on the journey, a time will come when he or she is confronted with a fresh decision that will help facilitate the process of becoming more like Jesus Christ. It is a period called the *Active Dark Night of the Spirit*. It differs from the Active Dark Night of the Senses, which was characterized by a sense of emptiness. The question in that period was, *"Where* are you, Lord?"

---

[42] II Corinthians 5:7
[43] Isaiah 40:3-5

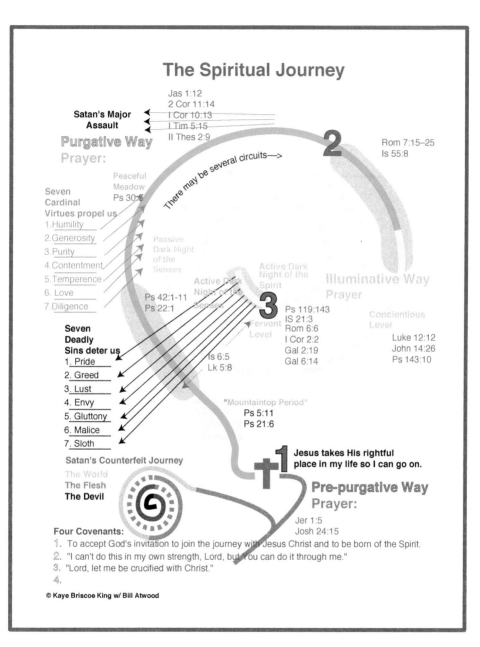

The Spiritual Journey

Jas 1:12
2 Cor 11:14

Satan's Major Assault
I Cor 10:13
I Tim 5:15
II Thes 2:9

Rom 7:15–25
Is 55:8

Purgative Way
Prayer:

There may be several circuits—>

Peaceful Meadow
Ps 30:5

Seven Cardinal Virtues propel us
1. Humility
2. Generosity
3. Purity
4. Contentment
5. Temperence
6. Love
7. Diligence

Passive Dark Night of the Senses

Active Dark Night of the Senses
Ps 42:1-11
Ps 22:1

Active Dark Night of the Spirit

Illuminative Way
Prayer

Ps 119:143
IS 21:3
Rom 6:6
I Cor 2:2
Gal 2:19
Gal 6:14

Concientious Level

Luke 12:12
John 14:26
Ps 143:10

Fervent Level

Seven Deadly Sins deter us
1. Pride
2. Greed
3. Lust
4. Envy
5. Gluttony
6. Malice
7. Sloth

Is 6:5
Lk 5:8

"Mountaintop Period"
Ps 5:11
Ps 21:6

Satan's Counterfeit Journey
The World
The Flesh
The Devil

Jesus takes His rightful place in my life so I can go on.

Pre-purgative Way
Prayer:
Jer 1:5
Josh 24:15

Four Covenants:
1. To accept God's invitation to join the journey with Jesus Christ and to be born of the Spirit.
2. "I can't do this in my own strength, Lord, but You can do it through me."
3. "Lord, let me be crucified with Christ."
4.

© Kaye Briscoe King w/ Bill Atwood

Now, the cry is one of discomfort as the holiness of God is manifest in our lives with great anguish. Now, the person says, "You are *here*, Lord, and you *see everything!*" It is at this point that we are convicted by our mixed motives and hypocrisy. For the individual, it seems like moving backwards. Their growth, however, is much more evident to friends and colleagues who are beside them.

Many pastors who move into this period of the journey find it very painful and are disillusioned by what is going on in their lives. Because they don't know that what is happening is "supposed to" happen, many clergy drop out of the ministry at this point. The great tragedy is that they are not failing but are actually being invited into deeper intimacy with God.

Something like a transfer of power takes place during the Active Dark Night of the Spirit. The pilgrim becomes increasingly dependent on the Lord for life and breath. For this to take place, the heart seeks to be crucified with Christ. Rather than the defensiveness we had in earlier stages of the journey, now the revelation of sin in our lives is welcomed. This is the third covenant intensified, when we cry, *"Lord, let my flesh be crucified."*

At a conference I attended a while back, several people came up to me during the day to say that they were having trouble dealing with one of the people at their table. He was being difficult and, they thought, petty because he insisted that certain aspects of the faith were more critical than others in the group perceived them to be. As the day progressed, they got more and more frustrated with him, and their complaints grew more numerous to me because he was overwhelming their indirect requests to lighten up. Finally, they asked me to speak with him. At the next break, as he was a close (if sometimes difficult!) friend of mine, I simply said, "A number of the people in your small group are frustrated. They think you are being a horse's rear end." When I told him, he looked at me with tenderness and said, "Thank you." In that moment, he showed the true character of his heart and also revealed where he was on the journey. He was actively seeking for any parts of his life that were out of order to be crucified with Christ. My comment to him was received not as an insult, but as the "wound of a friend."[44]

While this is very intentional, the next step is to move into transformation that takes place *without* our direct action (or even understanding). We move to become more and more like Jesus, even though we don't necessarily see it. When conformation to Him at the Spirit's initiative and action rather than by our decision and action occurs when we move into the ***Passive Dark Night of the Spirit.***

---

[44] Proverbs 27:6

Passive Dark Night of the Spirit

When I was a boy, we lived in Germany. Every Saturday, my brother and I rode the bus to the Army post to get a haircut, see a movie, and have lunch (all for $1.00 each!). At the movie theatre, we were always the last to arrive because the bus from where we lived arrived after everyone else was seated. Each week, before the feature film there was a shorter film called a serial because it was an ongoing story that unfolded a bit more each week. For more than a year, the serial was *Ace Drummond, Ace Aviator Battles the Evil Dr. Foo Manchu.* I can remember stopping in the entry of the theatre every week while the serial was just beginning. As the opening credits rolled, there was a close-up of my aviator hero, Ace, on the screen. Every week I said the same thing as I looked at the dashing adventurer on the screen, "Oh, Ace. I want to be like you! I'm gonna be like you!" (I've often wondered how much of a part that 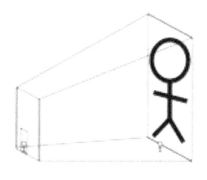 played in my later decision to be an Air Force pilot.)

Because we arrived so late, all the seats were filled except the front row. Week after week, we had to traipse through the theatre, row after row until we got to the front. From the front, next to the screen, my hero, who seemed to be life-size from the back, now seemed to be a giant. The picture was actually the same size as when I first came through the door, but my perspective had changed. Now that I was closer to the screen, he seemed too big for words. Every week, I said the same thing from the front of the theatre, "Oh Ace, I could never be like you!" It just seemed impossible to be that great.

Coming to know Jesus is something like that. When we first meet Him, from "the door of the theatre," He seems pretty easy to follow. After all, how hard could it be to be nice to children and pat lambs on the head? As we actually approach Him and get closer, it seems to us that we are going backward. He seems more holy, and it seems that we can never live up to what it means to bear His name. Because we are close, we look up to Him and see how magnificent He is and are utterly amazed at His holiness and how short we fall by comparison. We are confronted, painfully, with the truth that all *our* righteousness or righteous acts are "like filthy rags,"[45] compared to His holiness and righteousness. Others observing us can see that we are drawing closer, but we cannot

---

[45] Isaiah 64:6a

see it. This is why St. Paul could write, "This is a faithful saying and worthy of all acceptance, that Christ Jesus came into the world to save sinners, of whom I am chief."[46]

From our perspective, Paul was walking intimately with Jesus in a way we can only hope to emulate. From his, he was the worst sinner of all. It is because he was so close to the Holy One. The Dark Nights of the Spirit drive this.

Application
Being Crucified with Christ

1. During this time, we become acutely aware that *our* sins put Jesus Christ on the cross. The pain of that realization can be almost unbearable, especially as we consider the brutality. This can also be a time of beginning to comprehend the extent of the Lord's love for us, for it is in the realization of the anguish, of the piercing of His side, of the utter darkness and separation from the Father that we come to behold Him in a greater light, and to understand what He meant when He said that we are to love one another as He has loved us – that is part of becoming more like Him. How does His love for you change the way you look at others?

2. Have you entered that place of realizing that Jesus sees deep within the recesses of your soul? That *nothing* is hidden from Him? Have you come to recognize how desperately the flesh needs to be crucified so that Jesus can live His live through you? This is part of the Active Dark Night of the Spirit. What has the Holy Spirit revealed to you that needs to be crucified? Are you willing?

3. There are many things in our lives that are not friendly to our progressing to become more like Christ. Though He has won the ultimate victory, we are still called to be conformed to His character. God knows the desire of our hearts. You can cooperate with the process by praying a prayer like this:

Lord Jesus Christ, help me to become more like You. Help me remove anything that stands in the way of that process. Help crucify my flesh and help me be conformed to You.

---

[46] I Timothy 1:15

SECTION FOUR

THE UNITIVE WAY

CHAPTER SEVEN

Spiritual Betrothal and Marriage

As we begin to emerge from the Dark Nights of the Spirit, we are being prepared for Spiritual Union with the Lord. Things here are thought to occur in three stages. First, there is Spiritual Betrothal, then Spiritual Marriage, and at last Capacity, where we move into the fulfillment of our destiny in our relationship with Christ.

Spiritual Betrothal

It is probably not surprising that *Spiritual Betrothal* is very much like the parallel of preparing for marriage in normal human relationships. It is when we enter into a commitment that our union with Christ will become complete.

It is fascinating that Spiritual Betrothal is usually accompanied by a revelation of God in nature. The passage below from *Between the Soul and the Bridegroom* shows St. John's experience of God in the air, stream, meadow, and nightingale. What makes this passage particularly interesting is it is the fulfillment of an early, pre-purgative experience wherein people often feel closest to the God they have not yet actually met when they are in the beauty of nature.

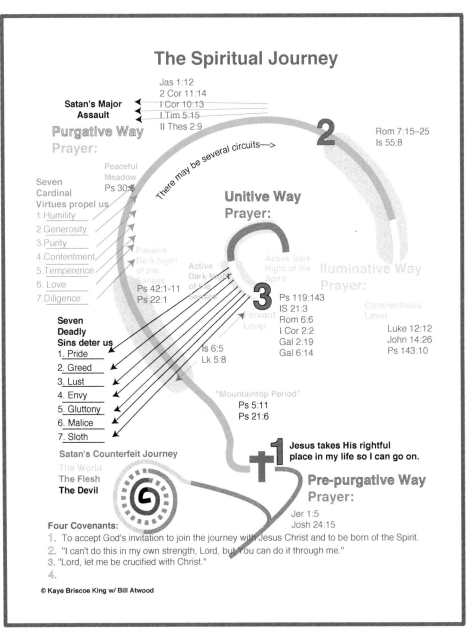

The Spiritual Journey

Satan's Major Assault
Jas 1:12
2 Cor 11:14
I Cor 10:13
I Tim 5:15
II Thes 2:9

Rom 7:15–25
Is 55:8

Purgative Way
Prayer:

There may be several circuits→

Peaceful Meadow
Ps 30:5

Seven Cardinal Virtues propel us
1. Humility
2. Generosity
3. Purity
4. Contentment
5. Temperence
6. Love
7. Diligence

Unitive Way
Prayer:

Passive Dark Night of the Senses
Ps 42:1-11
Ps 22:1

Active Dark Night of the Senses

Active Dark Night of the Spirit

Iluminative Way
Prayer:

Ps 119:143
IS 21:3
Rom 6:6
I Cor 2:2
Gal 2:19
Gal 6:14

Concientious Level

Luke 12:12
John 14:26
Ps 143:10

Fervent Level

Seven Deadly Sins deter us
1. Pride
2. Greed
3. Lust
4. Envy
5. Gluttony
6. Malice
7. Sloth

Is 6:5
Lk 5:8

"Mountaintop Period"
Ps 5:11
Ps 21:6

Satan's Counterfeit Journey
The World
The Flesh
The Devil

Jesus takes His rightful place in my life so I can go on.

Pre-purgative Way
Prayer:
Jer 1:5
Josh 24:15

Four Covenants:
1. To accept God's invitation to join the journey with Jesus Christ and to be born of the Spirit.
2. "I can't do this in my own strength, Lord, but You can do it through me."
3. "Lord, let me be crucified with Christ."
4.

© Kaye Briscoe King w/ Bill Atwood

The difference now is that the pilgrim knows the Lord. The pilgrim experiences something of the breadth of His character through His creation. This is not a vague experience of a faceless, nameless creator, however. It is a revelation of the heart of the One who has flung the stars across the heavens, heaped the mountains into statements of grandeur, molded oceans with a word, and populated the earth with a magnificent cornucopia of living things. The words of St. John of the Cross provide a beautiful description of this heavenly betrothal:

> Let us rejoice, Beloved,
> and let us go forth to behold ourselves in your beauty,
> to the mountain and to the hill,
> to where the pure water flows,
> and further, deep into the thicket.
>
> And then we will go on
> to the high caverns in the rock
> which are so well concealed;
> there we shall enter
> and taste the fresh juice of the pomegranates.
>
> There you will show me
> what my soul has been seeking,
> and then you will give me,
> you, my life, will give me there
> what you gave me on that other day:
>
> the breathing of the air,
> the song of the sweet nightingale,
> the grove and its living beauty
> in the serene night,
> with a flame that is consuming and painless. [47]

It is probably not surprising that Spiritual Betrothal is very much like the parallel of preparing for marriage in normal human relationships. It is when we enter into a commitment that our union with Christ will become complete.

A friend once confessed that he had regressed in his spiritual life. No longer was he spending hours on end in exhaustive intercession as he had done for years; now, he found himself fascinated by a family of wood ducks in his back yard. In the mornings, he would go out and watch them for hours through binoculars, sometimes praying in the spirit, sometimes just sitting in stillness and watching them.

---

[47] *Collected Works.* "Stanzas Between the Soul and the Bridegroom." Stanzas 36-39

At the heart of this change is a transformation of prayer life whereby we move from meditative prayer to contemplative. Whereas meditative prayer is focused on a passage or attribute of God as we search for new revelation, contemplative prayer is simply *being* with the One we love. We don't have to have a spiritual goal in mind or be able to articulate some spiritual "learning outcome" for having been with the Lord; we simply enjoy being with Him. Of course, this is what will fill eternity with Him.

Spiritual Marriage – The Fourth Covenant

From the beginning of creation, the heart of God has cried out to share his extravagant love. It is in the next step of *Spiritual Marriage* that we experience the quiet confidence of that relationship, as we await the richness of "knowing as we have been known" in union with Him. Many writers speak of this time in a kind of *knowing* code. St. John and St. Teresa talked about a revelation of the Trinity as something that usually accompanies the step of Spiritual Marriage. As with the earthly counterpart, spiritual marriage is the expression of the sweetest spiritual intimacies imaginable. It involves union so complete that it is hard to see where we stop and the Lord picks up. It is the utter confidence expressed by Paul, when he said, "For to me, to live is Christ, and to die *is* gain"[48] and " . . . I know whom I have believed and am persuaded that He is able to keep what I have committed to Him until that Day."[49]

People who have entered into Spiritual Marriage will, when asked about it, admit to having an experience revealing an apprehension of the Trinity at a level that was previously unknown. The interesting thing is they don't take the initiative to talk about it. There are two reasons for this. *First*, it is intensely personal. It is obviously tailored just for them and their lives. They understand that it would not be likely to make much sense if they were to share it. The *second* reason is that it is an experience that is essentially non-verbal so they don't have the words to share it.

They couldn't really share it if they wanted to. It is, however, intimate and sweet. The intimacy mirrors that in the best of our experience of intimate care and abandon in marriage. This is not to say that it is best described as physical intimacy, though the depth, freedom, and joy of the Lord has been wonderfully pre-figured in the joys of marital union. It is principally an application by faith of whom we are in Christ, which comes as a result of the third commitment, to be crucified with Him:

---

[48] Philippians 1:21
[49] II Timothy 1:12

> I have been crucified with Christ; it is no longer I who live, but Christ lives in me; and the life which I now live in the flesh I live by faith in the Son of God, who loved me and gave Himself for me.[50]

Spiritual union and marriage are reminiscent of a story of a little old couple that sits on the porch rocking side by side in two chairs. For a long time, they rock in silence, then one of them finally says, "I forget... Which one of us is it that doesn't like broccoli?" We become so lost in the Savior that our identity with Him blurs. That is true not only for us as we lose ourselves in Him, but other people see Jesus in us more and more clearly, too.

Application

1. Think of a specific time when you experienced something of the breadth of God's character through creation. How would you describe that moment? What was specifically meaningful to you?

2. Write a few paragraphs about your recent prayer times with the Lord. In contemplative prayer, we revel in simply spending time with God with no conversation, requests, or goals in mind. To what extent are you experiencing "contemplative" prayer? Has this become a natural portion of the journey, or are you still enjoying learning and discovering things in meditative prayer? Remember, there is no advantage in trying to rush ahead of where you are!

3. Have you made the decision to go beyond just appearing to be righteous to others and find your heart desire to truly be "crucified with Christ"? In other words, have you realized that all that you are and have already belong to God, and now you need to acknowledge His ownership of you and yield to His love? More than self-sacrifice, it is realizing how destructive the flesh is and truly desiring to die to self and live in the power of His Holy Spirit.

Lord Jesus, thank you that You opened the way to total surrender and submission when You submitted to the Father's will in the Garden. Thank you that your submission to the agony of the cross, followed by your glorious resurrection, provided the means for me to be reconciled to God, through You and to be changed into your likeness. Help me now, as I choose to submit all that I am and all that I have to You. Lead me, Lord, into the way of complete surrender and oneness with You.

---

[50] Galatians 2:20

CHAPTER EIGHT

Capacity – The Marriage Supper Anticipated

It might be natural to assume that the more mature in Christ a person becomes, the more obvious and sweeping their spiritual authority becomes. That is not entirely true. Whereas one can certainly see the maturity in the witness that Mother Theresa offered, it is not the case that because she was the "most mature" she was picked for the task of leading her order. It has to do with *"Capacity."* Capacity is the fulfillment of our destiny in Christ. There is need in the Kingdom of God for people who will live and minister with power. There is also need for those who will do so with tenderness.

If you think of the Lord as a source like a waterfall, our Capacity is like the design of a pipe that will determine how much water flows. It's not that only fire hoses are important. Little watering hoses for tender seedlings and newly sprouted plants need watering, too. It is not that one is more important than the other. It is just a question of what we are called to do.

Capacity in the Kingdom

Capacity is the fulfillment of our vocation and identity. It may occur in what appears to be obscurity, or it may be in the public eye. The choice belongs to God. The purpose is also to bring glory to His name, not attention to our lives. At this point, those in the **Unitive Way** are in such union with Christ that they have no interest in visibility. They want only to spend time with Jesus. It is that precise vocation that they know they will pursue for eternity when they leave this life for the next.

The Spiritual Journey

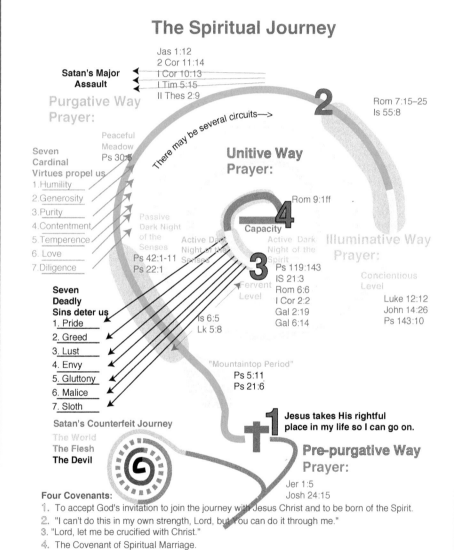

Satan's Major Assault

Jas 1:12
2 Cor 11:14
I Cor 10:13
I Tim 5:15
II Thes 2:9

Purgative Way Prayer:

Rom 7:15–25
Is 55:8

There may be several circuits—>

Peaceful Meadow
Ps 30:5

Seven Cardinal Virtues propel us
1. Humility
2. Generosity
3. Purity
4. Contentment
5. Temperence
6. Love
7. Diligence

Unitive Way Prayer:

Rom 9:1ff

Passive Dark Night of the Senses
Ps 42:1-11
Ps 22:1

Active Dark Night of the Senses

Capacity

Active Dark Night of the Spirit
Ps 119:143
IS 21:3
Rom 6:6
I Cor 2:2
Gal 2:19
Gal 6:14

Illuminative Way Prayer:

Concientious Level
Luke 12:12
John 14:26
Ps 143:10

Fervent Level
Is 6:5
Lk 5:8

Seven Deadly Sins deter us
1. Pride
2. Greed
3. Lust
4. Envy
5. Gluttony
6. Malice
7. Sloth

"Mountaintop Period"
Ps 5:11
Ps 21:6

Satan's Counterfeit Journey
The World
The Flesh
The Devil

Jesus takes His rightful place in my life so I can go on.

Pre-purgative Way Prayer:

Jer 1:5
Josh 24:15

Four Covenants:
1. To accept God's invitation to join the journey with Jesus Christ and to be born of the Spirit.
2. "I can't do this in my own strength, Lord, but You can do it through me."
3. "Lord, let me be crucified with Christ."
4. The Covenant of Spiritual Marriage.

Rather than appearing "super-spiritual," however, those in the Unitive Way seem to others to be pretty boring. They focus on the simple joys of prayer or creation. They speak with satisfaction about a piece of music, the state of their flower gardens, or how pleasant a meal with a friend has been. It can be frustrating for other members of the Body of Christ.

People in the Unitive Way move increasingly into introversion, choosing to live an interior life. They are simply not interested in things like church committees. It can be quite frustrating for pastors. People in the Unitive Way who are no longer interested in church work may well have been the ones who used to be the most fruitful workers when they were in the Illuminative Way. This is not to say that there is no ministry. There is a great ministry of fellowship with the Lord and a heart that gives rise to intercessions that are deep longings. Perhaps the most revealing of these prayers comes from St. Paul:

> For I could wish that I myself were accursed, *separated* from Christ for the sake of my brethren, my kinsmen according to the flesh, who are Israelites, to whom belongs the adoption as sons, and the glory and the covenants and the giving of the Law and the *temple* service and the promises, whose are the fathers, and from whom is the Christ according to the flesh, who is over all, God blessed forever. Amen.[51]

Notice what had happened: Paul had been so overtaken with the heart of Jesus that his prayer became the prayer of the Master. Although Paul could not actually restore someone else by virtue of becoming "accursed," his love for the Jews was so complete that his desire was to emulate the reconciling ministry of Jesus on the cross. Jesus was accursed for us and won for us redemption. Paul had so taken on the mind of Christ that he wanted to do what Jesus did. When one wonders about maturity, this is a good prayer to examine. Could we even conceive of giving up salvation for the sake of someone else? It is hard to even imagine. But so it is when we are consumed by His love.

Preparing for Eternity

Now, in the Unitive Way, the pilgrims are preparing for eternity. They surrender into the arms of the One they love and are stilled in their hearts. They have tasted eternity and are preparing (perhaps fully surrendered) to the Lord, even in death. For those in the Unitive Way, death is no longer such a big deal. Its assault has been vanquished by the promise that heaven is more real than the world around them. It will soon slip away, and life becomes filled with the quiet expectation that they will soon be

---

[51] Romans 9:3-5

with the Lord at the Marriage Supper of the Lamb. It is there the Church fulfills what each pilgrim has begun to know as an individual. They long for this union and seem to look far off to heaven with a sense of home-sickness. Things have developed to the place that eternity becomes more real than their lives here. It seems strange and distant and sort of mystic to the outside observer, but the Christian in the Unitive Way is not particularly concerned about what anyone else thinks. They know and can say with confidence:

> For I know *that* my Redeemer lives,
>   And He shall stand at last on the earth;
>   And after my skin is destroyed, this *I know,*
>   That in my flesh I shall see God,
>   Whom I shall see for myself,
>   And my eyes shall behold, and not a stranger.
>   *How* my heart yearns within me! [52]

After years of walking with the Lord, St. Theresa was reported to pray as her last breath, "O my Lord and my Spouse, the hour that I have so desired has come. It's time for us to meet one another."[53] We, too, may have that confidence. Those in the Unitive Way can sing, then, with those who have gone before, the words of Charles' Wesley's hymn:

> *No condemnation now I dread;*
> *Jesus, and all in Him, is mine;*
> *Alive in Him, my living Head,*
> *And clothed in righteousness divine,*
> *Bold I approach th'eternal throne,*
> *And claim the crown, through Christ my own.* [54]

---

[52] Job 19:25-27
[53] Thomas Alvarez, *The Prayers of St. Theresa of Avila* (New York: New City Press, 1990), 133.
[54] Charles Wesley, *Psalms and Hymns*, 1738.

Application

1.   The Unitive Way is not a place but a relationship. It is the fruit of decades of intimacy with the Lord. Most people who enter the Unitive Way do not think they are there. They are simply resting in the confidence that comes from having built a relationship of trust with the Lord.

Just as water takes on the character of tea when it is brewed, we can take on more and more of the character of Christ. Cultivating faithfulness will eventually yield a harvest. A joyous time awaits you; hence, you can give thanks to the Lord for where you are right now, knowing that He is guiding and leading you to this greater maturity in Him.

Thank you, Lord Jesus, for where I am right now! I know that You are with me, that You are guiding me, and that You have a place for me for all eternity that can begin in this life.   While we are together, help me to enjoy You and to welcome each day as a new adventure with You. Amen.

If you think you may have entered the "unitive way," you will be able to see some characteristics.

2. What has "decreased" so that He might "increase," to use John the Baptist's terms? Where do you see the increase of His life in your life?

3. How do you view the future? What longings do you have for "going home"?

Thank you, dear Lord, that I can say with Paul that to die is gain! I look forward to that day when You will come and receive me unto Yourself, that where You are, I may be also. In the meantime, I am grateful for the time I still have here and thank You for what You are doing in and through me as You are preparing a place for me. I pray that all that do and say would give glory to You alone. Amen.

SECTION FIVE

AFTERWORD

CHAPTER NINE

A Warning: The False Journey

Because we are frail and have an enemy who has as his main aim "to steal, kill, and destroy"[55] all who would follow Jesus, we must be ever mindful of the potential for getting on the wrong path of a false journey.

The False Journey

At the heart of the false journey is not an indictment that people want to "go wrong"; instead, it is the natural (though sad) desire not to have to change. It is a beguiling siren song that says, "Come as you are and stay as you are." It is vastly different from the Christian Gospel that says, "Come as you are and be transformed into the image of Christ."[56]

Tragically, this is the heart of the "revisionist gospel." In an effort to be as welcoming as possible, those who have been seduced by a message that requires no change slip further and further into the darkness. Like the boys' island in the story of Pinocchio as rebellious children more fully embrace their fantasies, they become donkeys.[57] It is a wonderful image. As people cast off restraint and move into a world without boundaries, there is nothing to stop them from making utter fools of themselves. Sadly, the change comes at a pace that is easily missed.

As sons and daughters of Adam and Eve, we have been deeply

---

[55] John 10:10
[56] Romans 8:29, II Corinthians 3:18
[57] Carlo Collodi, *The Adventures of Pinocchio* (1883).

impacted by the sin of the Garden. We have eaten of the same fruit of the tree of the knowledge of good and evil, and we have decided for ourselves what is good and what is bad. Sadly, our conviction does not always line up with God's. When that happens, it is not He who is off track.

Rather than taking an air of superiority toward Adam and Eve in the garden, a close look at the scene shows that they were bombarded in their senses with temptations from every direction. Look at these verses and the clever way that the devil used the deadly sins to lure them.

Gen. 3:2 The woman said to the serpent, "From the fruit of the trees of the garden we may eat;
Gen. 3:3 but from the fruit of the tree which is in the middle of the garden, Go has said, 'You shall not eat from it or touch it, or you will die.'"
Gen. 3:4 The serpent said to the woman, "You surely will not die!

Malice. Possibly resenting God's rule

Gen. 3:5 "For God knows that in the day you eat from it your eyes will be opened, and you will be like God, knowing good and evil."

Pride. Seeing themselves as equal with God
Envy. Wanting what God had
Sloth. Finding an easy way to get knowledge
Covet. Wanting what was not theirs

Gen. 3:6 When the woman saw that the tree was good for food, and that it was a delight to the eyes, and that the tree was desirable to make one wise, she took from its fruit and ate; and she gave also to her husband with her, and he ate.

Gluttony. Want food they didn't need
Lust. Delighting in what was forbidden

Embracing the World

The beginning of the false journey sneaks up on a person. We don't know that we have a problem. Like the imposing matron who faced the end of her life in the classic film *Good Morning, Miss Dove,* many people have little sense of having been on the wrong track. As the aging spinster comes to the end of her life, having taught generations of children, she announces to her parish priest, "You know, I do **not** find the 'burden of my sins intolerable.'" That may be partly due to the fact that she thought she lived a relatively upright life, but it also speaks to the fact that she had almost no understanding of the holiness of God.

Perhaps one of the most beguiling steps that one may take to get started on the false journey is to say, "I'm not so bad." Conveniently, there is always someone else around who can serve as a bad example—someone who is less upright, or at least less skilled at masking sin.

At this stage of the false journey, the ravages of sin have not yet brought forth their full harvest. Many are able to rationalize and overlook what is actually occurring, taking refuge in the subtle encouragement from the dark side that they need not face either hard choices or change.

As a common illustration describes it, we can be like a frog put in a pot of water on the stove. As the heat is applied and the water begins to warm gradually, the frog is not aware of the change occurring in the environment – until it is too late: he has been boiled to death. Similarly, unless we are vigilant in our spiritual lives, we can become so immersed in the social, political, and religious environments that redefine what is morally or spiritually right that we begin to be absorbed by them.

As the beginning pilgrims on the Spiritual Journey are being grounded in Christ, those in the early steps of the false journey embrace relativism and/or the prosperity gospel, which offers material, rather than spiritual, growth. In relativism, the key is not the apprehension of absolute truth, but of *pluriformity*. The phrase *pluriform truth* has been one of the hallmarks of the revisionist leaders of the church. Rather than being boxed in by absolutes, they seek to provide a path to liberation by looking at things from different angles and perspectives and readily offering explanations. In doing so, they actually have joined the one who proclaimed, "I will ascend above the heights of the clouds, I will be like the Most High,"[58] for they have rejected the truth of God and substituted instead their own truth, thereby making themselves their own authority, or god. The other temptation to a false gospel is what is called the *prosperity gospel*, which proclaims that God wants you to be happy, healthy, and wealthy. Nothing could be more distinct from what our Lord said: "If anyone desires to come after Me, let him deny himself, and take up his cross, and follow Me."[59]

There are, of course, other false journeys, among them many cults that profess to be Christian. Addressing those matters is beyond the scope of this present book. One warning that is helpful, however, is to ask of those groups the same question Jesus posed to his disciples: "Whom do you say that I am?" If the answer is other than the second Person of the Triune

---

[58] Isaiah 14:14
[59] Matthew 16:14, Mark 8:34, Luke 9:13

Godhead, then you know that their way is a false gospel.

In closing, the prayer of the writer to the Hebrews seems appropriate:

> Now may the God of peace who brought up our Lord Jesus from the dead, that great Shepherd of the sheep, through the blood of the everlasting covenant, make you complete in every good work to do His will, working in you what is well pleasing in His sight, through Jesus Christ, to whom be glory forever and ever. Amen.[60]

---

[60] Hebrews 13:20

Application

1. Have you ever gotten off the right path and fallen into the enemy's snare? How did the enemy's "siren song" lure you from the Way, the Truth, and the Life? Identifying that can help you avoid being trapped in the future.

2. Have you ever fallen victim to the lie that says, "I'm really not so bad"? When and how did the subtleties of the enemy's lie(s) gain a foothold? How do you think you can turn the excursion on a false path back to the path of life?

3. Have you been deceived by a teaching or cult that denies the Person and work of Jesus Christ? Some teaching tries to lure people toward a material "prosperity gospel" instead of into true Kingdom abundance, where the fruit of the Spirit is what is emphasized. How can you identify false teaching?

3. If you have ever gone astray, what specifically made you realize that you were going the wrong direction?

4. Be careful! Those who think they will not stumble are terribly vulnerable. The best way to insure fidelity is having relationships of accountability. Who is in your life with whom you can be completely honest about where you are and what you have done? With whom are you in a relationship that is so firmly rooted in Christ that you can speak life to them when they are on the wrong path?

Lord Jesus, I confess that I have succumbed to the enemy's lies and snares by _____. *I ask You to forgive me and thank You that I can have the confidence of knowing that your blood washes away all my sins and that, as I confess them, You are faithful to forgive all my sins and to cleanse me of all unrighteousness. Thank You that I am washed whiter than snow and that You remember my sins no more. I also forgive anyone who has played a part in my "detour" off the path of righteousness. I thank you that it is your purpose, as the Good Shepherd, to get me, a wayward sheep, back on the right path, and that in this moment, You are doing so. With all those who have experienced this faithfulness on Your part, I sing" hallelujah, what a Savior!"*

Personal Notes

CPSIA information can be obtained
at www.ICGtesting.com
Printed in the USA
LVOW02s1515121016
508365LV00006BA/29/P